PRAISE FOR BETTER AGILE

"This is the book I've been looking for: a short, straightforward guide to agile for the 2020s. David cuts through the detail and tells you what you need to look at to upgrade your team to better ways of working."

–Allan Kelly, Agile coach, acclaimed multi-book author, and co-founder of the Agile on the Beach conference

"What can you do to continuously improve your agility? In this book, David distils the essentials of agile into practical, useful and interesting tools that will guide any leader towards improvements. The coaching questions provide a simple yet profound technique to take you to the next level of effectiveness."

–Javier Ponce Suarez, Group VP Head of Digital Transformation at Atos

"Ever since I have known David, he has always been leading the charge for making software delivery more agile. In this book he lays out the key lessons he has learned from that mission, in a way that is straightforward and easy-to-understand for us all."

–Rob Price, Director, Alchemmy Digital and Founder of Corporate Digital Responsibility

"I love what David's achieved here. By walking through the core agile concepts and practices, this book builds into a comprehensive guide to improving your teams. David has coupled this insight with deep practicality you can apply today. If you're new to running Agile software teams, then start here! If you're experienced at running teams, but are not seeing the improvements you'd hoped for, jump straight into the coaching questions and self-diagnose your way to the next level."

–Chris Baynham-Hughes, Open Transformation Principal at Red Hat Open Innovation Labs

"Whenever David presents at agile events, he radiates his deep passion, energy and expertise for all things agile. This wonderful book does the same and is guaranteed to inspire and support teams to take their agility to the next level!"

–Tom James, Technical Product Manager at Comparethemarket.com and organiser of the Agile Northants meetup

"Better Agile is the perfect companion for delivering a smooth agile transformation. With its 55 coaching questions, it can help all team members adopt a more agile approach, so they can find satisfaction in finally focussing on what brings value. Bring this book with you to every retrospective!"

–Catherine Lequibain, Global Agile Coach at Worldline

"A practical, straight-to-the-point book full of specific advice you'll be able to put into practice immediately. The concepts discussed here are essential – David not only gets you to understand the whys and hows of agile software development, but he does so in a way that is quick and easy to understand."

–Dr Andreas Oikonomou, Senior Lecturer in Computing at Nottingham Trent University

BETTER AGILE

HOW EVERY SOFTWARE TEAM CAN SPEND
LESS TIME FIREFIGHTING AND HAVE MORE
FUN BUILDING GREAT SOFTWARE

DAVID DALY

Copyright © 2022 David Daly

First Edition

All rights reserved. No part of this book may be reproduced or used in any manner without the prior written permission of the copyright owner, except for the use of brief quotations in a book review.

ISBN: 979-8-4149-0646-9 (Hardcover)

ISBN: 979-8-4144-4836-5 (Paperback)

Disclaimer Notice:

Every effort has been made to ensure the information in this book was correct at the time of publication, but the author does not assume any liability for loss or damage, direct or indirect, which is incurred as a result of the use of the information contained within this book, including, but not limited to, errors, omissions or inaccuracies.

Cover illustration: iStock.com/Jesussanz

CONTENTS

Introduction	11
1. AGILE SECRET #1: OPTIMISE FOR FLOW	**17**
Why optimise for flow?	17
The software development lifecycle	18
Touch time vs. wait time	19
Queues and batch sizes	21
Bottlenecks	27
Blockers	31
Rework	33
Key takeaways	36
Further reading	37
References	38
2. AGILE SECRET #2: GET THE RIGHT PEOPLE DOING THE RIGHT THINGS	**39**
Why get the right people doing the right things?	39
Prioritisation	40
Self-selection	45
Key takeaways	50
Further reading	51
References	52
3. AGILE SECRET #3: SHORTEN FEEDBACK LOOPS	**53**
Why shorten feedback loops?	53
Feedback from builds	54
Feedback from testing	55
Feedback from customers	58
Feedback from end-users	62
Feedback about team effectiveness	64
Information radiators	68

Metrics 70
Key takeaways 71
Further reading 72
References 73

4. 10-MINUTE SCRUM OVERVIEW 75
Overview of Scrum 75
Why Scrum works 77
Further reading 80

5. 5 SCRUM MISTAKES TO AVOID 81
Mistake #1: Water-Scrum-Fall 81
Mistake 2: Multi-sprint stories 82
Mistake 3: Ineffective Product Owner 83
Mistake 4: Not reaching a potentially shippable state in every Sprint 85
Mistake #5: Ignoring required technical practices 86
References 87

6. 10-MINUTE KANBAN OVERVIEW 89
Overview of Kanban 89
Why Kanban works 94
Further reading 98
References 99

7. 5 KANBAN MISTAKES TO AVOID 101
Mistake #1: Task-board only 101
Mistake #2: Not limiting WIP 102
Mistake #3: Not starting with what you do now 103
Mistake #4: No feedback loops 104
Mistake #5: Mapping who does the work rather than the value-adding steps 105

8. HOW TO CHOOSE BETWEEN SCRUM AND KANBAN 107
Why choose Scrum? 108
Why choose Kanban? 109
Scrumban – the best of both worlds? 109

9. 5-MINUTE AGILITY SELF-ASSESSMENT	111
How to assess your team's agility in 5 minutes	111
Self-assessment questions	112
10. RECAP OF COACHING QUESTIONS	119
Optimise for flow	119
Get the right people doing the right things	121
Shorten feedback loops	122
Notes	125
Acknowledgments	127
About the Author	129

INTRODUCTION

If you're anything like me, or the hundreds of other software engineers, development managers, agile coaches, and executives that I have worked with over my 20+ years in tech, you have probably noticed that everyone expects software teams to:

- Deliver new features faster to be able to adapt more quickly to new expectations from customers
- Build software that is bug-free and always available
- Create user experiences that are brilliantly intuitive

Yet, at the same time, in many companies, these same teams are stretched to the limit, and there is simply no time or budget to do things like:

- Re-write or re-architect code to reduce technical debt
- Try out new ways of working to make the team more effective
- Attend training courses to learn new skills
- Bring in external consultants or coaches to help the team improve

I am lucky enough to have built up many years of experience leading and coaching software development teams, lecturing at universities, speaking at agile events, and working closely with agile coaches and business leaders. This has given me the chance to see first-hand what works and creates positive outcomes, as well as the common pitfalls and obstacles that teams often face.

In this book, I have condensed this experience into the essential information you need to make agile work better for your team, no matter what your starting point is.

In this book you will find:

- **The three essential secrets of how to make agile work for you.** Whether you are using Scrum, Kanban, SAFe, LeSS, or any other method or framework, these three secrets explain the fundamental principles that are key to every successful agile implementation. By understanding them, you will immediately be able to spot the best ways to boost your team's agility.

- **10-minute overviews of Scrum and Kanban.** These are the most popular agile development methods, and these quick overviews will show you how to achieve the best results when you apply them.
- **Common mistakes to avoid.** By explaining the five most common mistakes I have seen teams making when they try to use Scrum or Kanban, you can save yourself time and stress by learning from other people's mistakes rather than your own.
- **A simple way to decide between Scrum and Kanban.** One of the questions I have most often been asked is whether to choose Scrum or Kanban. In just a few pages I explain how you can make the best choice for your situation, including the option of using both!
- **A 5-minute agility self-assessment.** This simple but powerful questionnaire consists of ten questions and takes just five minutes to complete. It immediately tells you which things you could change to give your team the most benefit with the least amount of effort.
- **55 of the best coaching questions you can ask yourself or your team to drive change.** All good coaches would agree that the best way to drive change is by asking the right questions rather than by telling people what to do. That's why, throughout this book, I have included the key questions you can ask yourself or those around

you in order to trigger improvements. I have also brought all of these coaching questions together in the final chapter to provide a handy day-to-day reference.
- **Recommended further reading.** This is a short book. I know most software engineers, development managers and executives don't have the time to read and digest hundreds of pages just to find one or two pieces of actionable advice. However, if you do want to go into more depth, I share with you the books that I have personally read and would recommend, if you want to learn more.

When I started my career in software, I was convinced that most of the approaches being used at the time (mostly waterfall projects delivering against fixed requirements) could be improved upon. Not only were these waterfall projects often not delivering good business outcomes, they were also no fun for the people working on them, frequently resulting in stress and burn-out.

Now, I think everyone recognises that agile software development is a better approach, yet many still fail to get the benefits they hope for when they adopt an agile method or technique. For example, I've seen cases where people adopt specific practices, like a "daily stand-up" or a "Kanban board", but don't see any improvements. I've also seen whole teams sent on a Scrum training course, but very little actually changing as a result.

Armed with this book, you will be able to figure out the action you need to take to make agile work better for you – ultimately giving you more time to craft great software which delights your customers, whilst also having a lot more fun in the process!

CHAPTER 1
AGILE SECRET #1: OPTIMISE FOR FLOW

WHY OPTIMISE FOR FLOW?

Are people on your team overloaded? Are they multi-tasking to extreme levels? Are some people so busy that you must wait several weeks for them to complete even small tasks? Are changes often blocked, waiting for someone or something? Are people spending as much time (or more) fixing things that are broken rather than implementing new features?

If any of these sound familiar, then you will benefit from optimising for flow.

In this chapter, I will explain:

- How to calculate your flow efficiency and why it matters

- Why you need to reduce batch sizes if you want to reduce lead times
- How to focus on bottlenecks so that you get the most improvements for the least amount of effort
- How to reduce the frequency and impact of blockers that lead to delays
- Why you need to shorten feedback loops to reduce the cost of rework

THE SOFTWARE DEVELOPMENT LIFECYCLE

As a software change goes from an initial idea through to working feature(s) that are live in production, it moves through a series of stages known as the end-to-end software development life-cycle (or SDLC). I like to think of each stage as adding some value: gradually refining the initial idea until it is concretely manifested as live software that is being used. Typical stages might be[1]:

- Propose a requirement (Product Manager)
- Document the requirement (Business Analyst)
- Sign-off the requirement (Product Manager)
- Design a feature to meet the requirement (Software Designer)
- Code and unit test a software change that implements the feature and integrate it with other software changes (Developer)
- Build a release and deploy it to a test environment (Release Engineer)
- Perform system testing (Tester)

- Deliver the change into the production environment (Production Engineer)
- Verify the change in production (Customer/End-Users)

For now, to simplify the explanations that follow, I'm assuming that each stage is the responsibility of a different person or team (as indicated in brackets). Later, in Chapter 7, I'll show you that these stages do not have to map onto specific people or teams, and why there are benefits to having individual people or teams carrying out some or all of the stages.

Coaching Questions

- If you don't already have it, can you make a list of the main steps that a software change goes through in your organisation to go from the initial idea right through to it being live in production?

TOUCH TIME VS. WAIT TIME

To move a software change through each of these stages requires effort. The time spent on these activities is called *touch time*[2]. Time when the change is not being actively worked on is known as *wait time*. The total *lead time* (sometimes called *elapsed time*) to deliver a software change is the sum of touch time and wait time.

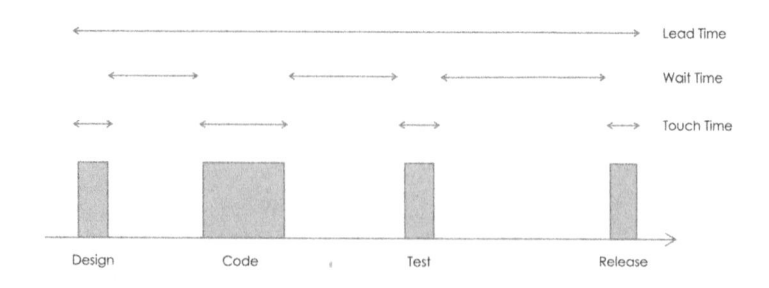

Touch time, wait time and lead time

The ratio of touch time to lead time is the *flow efficiency*. For knowledge work (including software development), it is not uncommon to see a ratio of around 1:10 for touch time to lead time (Anderson, 2010), and I have seen cases where flow efficiency is as low as 2.5%. What should be clear from this is that usually the most effective way to reduce the total lead time is to reduce wait time. For most teams, a 10% reduction in wait time, will have a much bigger impact than halving the time it takes to actually work on a software change.

Coaching Questions

- Can you find out or estimate your team's flow efficiency (ratio of touch time to lead time)?
- What are some of the main causes of wait time that you can identify?
- Are handovers between different people or teams exacerbating wait time?

QUEUES AND BATCH SIZES

So why is there typically such a high percentage of wait time? One of the biggest causes is having large batch sizes (the others are bottlenecks and blockers, which I'll cover shortly).

When you look at the example stages for delivering a software change listed earlier, you can see that it is possible to batch together software changes at each of these steps. For example, it is very usual to group together a set of requirements to be approved by a customer before work is started. Similarly, at the other end of the process, it is common practice to release multiple changes into production at the same time (usually based on a release schedule).

In "Managing the Design Factory", Donald. G. Reinertsen observed that whenever you place a large batch process before a small batch process, queues will inevitably form (Reinertsen, 1998). He gives the example of an aeroplane arriving at an airport (large batch process) and all passengers having to have their passports checked (small batch process). The large batch of people arriving at one time causes queues because passport control can only process a few people at a time. The conclusion: try to avoid having large batch sizes in your process upstream of smaller batch sizes. Understanding what your batch sizes are and where they are causing queues is an incredibly powerful tool for reducing lead times.

Let's work through a software example. First, take the case where software changes are developed continuously, followed by two large batch steps: system testing and release. You can see that the average lead time for a change is from halfway through development to the completion of the release.

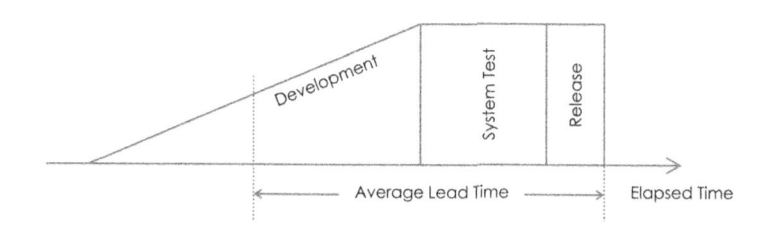

System Test and Release in Batches

If you adapt your ways of working, so that system testing is performed continuously as software changes are completed, you will see that (in theory) there is no reduction in average lead time (which is still limited by the large-batch release at the end of the process). That is not to say that there aren't many advantages to continuous testing. In practice, the shortened feedback cycles will increase efficiency and hence reduce lead times. But such lead time improvements are not a direct effect of reducing the batch size for system testing.

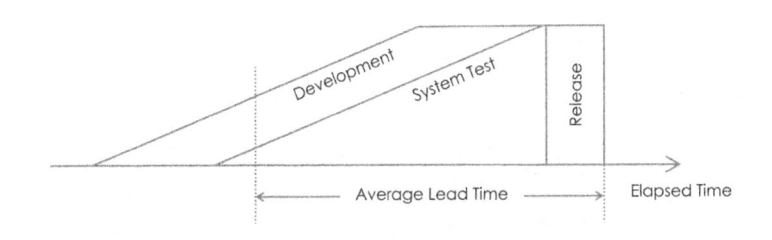

Continuous System Test

Now let's add requirements analysis and sign-off into the mix. If you do this continuously, you will see that the overall lead time is extended roughly in proportion to how long it takes to analyse one requirement.

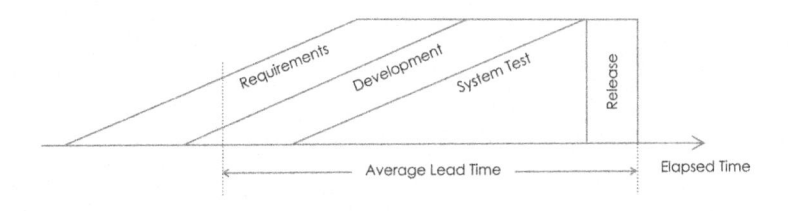

Continuous Requirements

However, if analysing and signing-off requirements is managed as a large batch, then the impact on the overall lead time is much greater (and out of proportion with the actual effort involved in analysing each requirement).

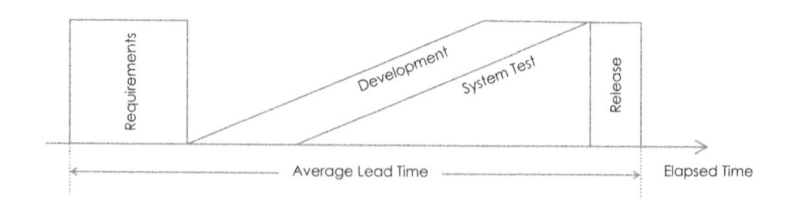

Batch Requirements

So you can see that, just like in the airport example, it is the positioning of a large batch process *before* a continuous process that leads to more wait time (which negatively impacts flow efficiency and increases average lead times).

Taking it one step further, if you can make all parts of the process continuous, then you will achieve the best average lead time.

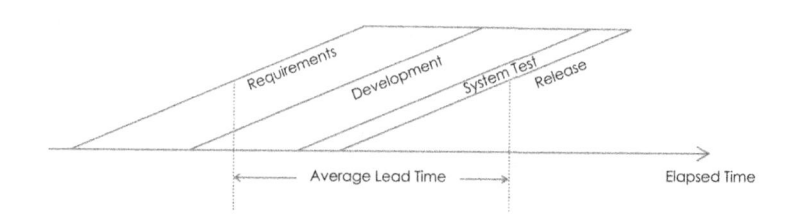

Fully Continuous Software Development

Coaching Questions

- Can you identify where the large batch transfers occur in your end-to-end software delivery process?
- Are they before small batch processes?
- Do they lead to queues?
- How could you reduce these batch sizes?

As you can see from these examples, when looking at the end-to-end software development life-cycle, optimising for flow involves minimising batch sizes. At the extreme, *single-piece flow* is where a new software change is only started as another one is completed. In other words, the rate at which work begins on new requirements exactly matches the rate of changes being released into production. This doesn't mean that only one change is being worked on at any one time, just that there is no more than one change at any one step in the process at any one time.

A concept that is related to batch size is *Work In Progress* (usually shortened to WIP). In simple terms, WIP is the number of software changes that have been started but not yet completed. High WIP creates a lot of wait time and hence longer lead times. Low WIP reduces wait time and hence gives shorter lead times. WIP also has a relationship to staff utilisation (the percentage of their time spent on value-adding tasks). Higher WIP increases utilisation whereas lower WIP decreases utilisation. Technically, choosing the right WIP level should be based upon how you want to balance the optimisation of lead time versus the optimisation of utilisation. Practically though, for almost every team I have ever worked with, WIP is too high. In the majority of cases, teams can significantly reduce WIP and improve lead times without making their utilisation worse. A rule-of-thumb that I have found will yield improvements for most teams is to limit WIP to 2-3 software changes per team member. In the chapter about Kanban, I'll also explain in more detail how to visualise and limit WIP and what the benefits are of doing so.

Coaching Questions

- Do you already track the WIP of your team?
- If not, can you measure or estimate your team's current WIP levels?
- Is it more than 2-3 changes per person?
- If so, what are the main causes for it being higher?
- Could you experiment with introducing WIP limits?

BOTTLENECKS

Every software development life-cycle has one bottleneck. The bottleneck is the single stage in the process that is limiting the overall throughput of software changes. In our example process, let's assume there is one person who completes all software designs (converting an approved requirement into a specification for a feature). If they cannot keep up with the rate at which requirements are being identified, documented and signed-off, and if all downstream activities are able to complete the remaining stages at a faster rate than the designer, then the design step is the bottleneck. Note: I have always found it more helpful to talk about bottlenecks in the life-cycle, rather than describing individual people or roles as a bottleneck.

The rate at which work moves through the whole process will be limited by (and be exactly the same as) the rate that work moves through the bottleneck. Making any other part of the process faster will have no impact on the end-to-end delivery rate. Only improvements impacting the bottleneck will improve your end-to-end performance. This is known as the *Theory of Constraints* which was first described by Eliyahu M. Goldratt in his business novel "The Goal" (Goldratt, 2004).

Queues are often a good (and easy) way to identify bottlenecks. There will always be a big queue before a bottleneck, and there will always be people waiting for work after a bottleneck. Unfortunately, in some organisations, everyone is so overloaded (and the process is so clogged up) that it can be difficult to even discern where the bottleneck actually is, because there are queues everywhere. This is another reason why limiting WIP is useful: it is much easier to find bottlenecks when WIP is managed. I rather like how Håkan Forss equated this to lowering the water level so that you can see where the rocks are (Forss, 2014).

Coaching Questions

- Do you have an idea of where the bottleneck in your software development life-cycle might be?
- How could you confirm or disprove this?

The Theory of Constraints recommends three strategies for alleviating bottlenecks and describes them (in order of preference) as:

1. Exploit the bottleneck
2. Subordinate everything else to the bottleneck
3. Elevate the bottleneck

I have never found this terminology intuitive, so let me try to explain each one of them in the context of our example, and also provide some simpler language that you can use to communicate these ideas more easily to other people.

Exploiting the bottleneck means *increasing focus*. In our example, this would mean taking steps to ensure that the person creating the software designs is able to focus as much of their energy as possible on that task. This could be achieved in any number of ways, for example:

- Reducing interruptions
- Freeing them from any tasks not related directly to software design (e.g. admin)
- Ensuring they have all the tools and information they need

It could even mean identifying certain types of changes where a design is not needed. Remember, even if introducing these measures makes other people working on other steps in the process less productive, that will not have a negative impact on end-to-end performance because end-to-end performance is only limited by the bottleneck and nothing else.

Subordinating everything else to the bottleneck means *increasing support*. This is achieved by reducing the throughput of other steps in the process to match the throughput of the bottleneck, and then using that spare capacity to support the bottleneck. In our example, this could mean developers taking on some design tasks. It can also mean finding ways of avoiding unnecessary work for the designer. For example, low quality requirements may result in greater effort for the designer. Or it may be that some requirements are approved but then abandoned after development has started. Any effort spent by the software designer on changes that are later dropped, is entirely wasted. Adding work upstream (such as additional checks) to reduce the likelihood of this waste will improve overall throughput.

Elevating the bottleneck means *increasing capacity*. This can mean adding people (e.g. recruiting another software designer), but there are also other ways of increasing capacity. Perhaps by learning new skills or by being equipped with better tooling, the designer's capacity can be enhanced. Automation can be used as a way to elevate a bottleneck (although more usually for testing, build and deployment activities). The reason that elevating the bottleneck is the "last resort" is that usually it is a relatively time consuming and costly option when compared with exploiting the bottleneck or subordinating everything else to it.

One thing you will have noticed by now, is that many of the approaches to alleviating the bottleneck involve changes to other parts of the process, rather than changes that directly involve the bottleneck itself.

Often you will find that, having alleviated the bottleneck, you discover a new bottleneck elsewhere in the process. When this happens, you can apply the Theory of Constraints again for the new bottleneck, in order to iteratively improve further.

Coaching Questions

- Can you think of how your team might alleviate the bottleneck in your process?
- Can you think of one or more ideas in each category (exploit, subordinate, elevate)?

BLOCKERS

I think of anything that prevents a software change from being actively worked on as a *blocker*. Examples include waiting for someone on the team to become available to work on a change, waiting for another team to deliver something (e.g. server hardware, development or test environments, network connectivity, etc.), or even that the change cannot be completed until another related change is finished first.

A bottleneck will often cause software changes to be blocked, but a bottleneck is rarely the only source of blockers. All blockers reduce flow efficiency and hence increase end-to-end lead times. My experience is that teams who take proactive steps to manage blockers achieve better flow.

Coaching Questions

- How does your team currently manage blockers?
- Is this approach effective?
- Are blockers resolved swiftly enough?

One very useful practice is to make blocked items visible. Some teams use a physical whiteboard to manage their work and they stick a brightly coloured post-it note with a description of the blocker onto the item that is blocked. Some software packages allow virtual post-it notes representing work-items to visibly "age" the longer the work-item that it represents stays in one step in the process. Another approach is to mark a dot next to a post-it note for every day that it stays in the same step in the process. I am still surprised how often just the practice of identifying work-items that are blocked and making this visible to the team is enough to ensure that the team takes action to unblock them.

Going one step further, teams who spend some time analysing which blockers occur most frequently and why, can take steps to reduce their incidence in the future. For example, one team I worked with found their network connectivity to be very unreliable. Fixing the network connectivity was outside of their scope of control, but what they could do was reduce their reliance on it (through the extensive use of virtual machines and distributed version control) to ensure that work did not become blocked when the network dropped out.

Coaching Questions

- What frequently occurring source of blockers exists for your team?
- What could you change to reduce the delay caused by these sources of blockers in the future?

REWORK

Rework describes any remediation work that is needed to fix something that was not done right in the first place. It is sometimes also referred to as CONQ (Cost of Non-Quality). I find it extremely useful to use a broad definition of rework. At one end of the spectrum, for example, would be a case where a developer tweaks some code, hits the compile button, and the compilation fails. That developer then has to rework the code until it compiles successfully. At the opposite end of the spectrum, an example might be a feature that needs to be completely rewritten because it did not achieve the intended benefits. Sometimes even features that correctly address the documented requirements, are implemented elegantly, and are free from bugs, still fail to deliver the value that was expected.

Based on research (Jones, 2000) David Anderson estimated that it is "common for teams to spend 90% of their available capacity on defect fixes" (Anderson, 2010). I also recognise this from my personal experience of working with software teams. What this means is that, in the same way that reducing wait time will have the biggest impact on lead time, reducing rework will, for most teams, have the single biggest impact on productivity. But rework is not only a drain on productivity, it also negatively impacts the flow of the entire development life-cycle. Developers have to stop working on one change to fix a problem that has been found during system testing. System testers have to stop testing the next release to reproduce an issue that has been found in production. Rework doesn't only negatively impact the lead time for the software change that needs the fixing, it also negatively impacts the lead time for other changes as well.

In general, the cost of rework increases the longer the time is between the error being introduced and it being discovered. In our previous example, the effort needed for the developer to correct some code until it compiles is far lower than the effort needed to completely redesign and implement a feature because the initial attempt did not achieve the intended benefits. There are many ways that feedback loops can be shortened. At a technical level, this could be by running a full suite of automated unit tests after making each code change. At a more organisational level, having developers sit next to (or at least be in close communication with) business stakeholders, can reduce the likelihood of a change not achieving the intended benefits. In Chapter 3 I cover a lot more about the different types of feedback loops you need to have in place and how to shorten them.

Coaching Questions

- Can you estimate what percentage of time your team spends on rework?
- How could this rework be avoided?
- How could you shorten feedback cycles so that the cost of rework is lowered?

KEY TAKEAWAYS

- Optimising for flow means increasing flow efficiency by reducing batch sizes, managing bottlenecks and blockers, and minimising rework
- Flow efficiency is touch time divided by lead time
- Reducing batch sizes reduces overall lead time, especially when large batches occur before a continuous process
- Use the Theory of Constraints to identify and alleviate bottlenecks by increasing focus, support and/or capacity
- Understand common sources of blockers on your team and find ways to reduce the delay they cause
- Shorten feedback cycles to reduce the effort spent on rework

FURTHER READING

The Goal: A Process of Ongoing Improvement by Eliyahu M. Goldratt

This is the book in which Eliyahu M. Goldratt first set out his Theory of Constraints. Although it is not written about software development, it is a "business novel" which makes it a pleasant, easy read. You do, however, have to make some effort to think about how these principles can be applied to software engineering.

Managing the Design Factory by Donald Reinertsen

This classic book describes how to optimise the design of (non-software) products (which I think has many more parallels to software development than, say, a car factory production line). In particular, it contains an excellent explanation of the importance and impact of batch sizes.

REFERENCES

Anderson, D. J. (2010). Kanban: Successful Evolutionary Change for Your Technology Business. Blue Hole Press.

Forss, H. (2014). How to improve Flow Efficiency with Scrum. Retrieved from https://hakanforss.wordpress.com/2014/08/18/how-to-improve-flow-efficiency-with-scrum-agile2014-qa/

Goldratt, E. M. (2004). The Goal: A Process of Ongoing Improvement (3rd Ed). Routledge.

Jones, C. (2000). Software Assessments, Benchmarks, and Best Practices. Addison-Wesley Professional.

Reinertsen, D. G. (1998). Managing the Design Factory: A Product Developers Tool Kit. Free Press.

CHAPTER 2
AGILE SECRET #2: GET THE RIGHT PEOPLE DOING THE RIGHT THINGS

WHY GET THE RIGHT PEOPLE DOING THE RIGHT THINGS?

Are people not focussed on the most important work that needs to be done? Are there not enough people with particular skills? Are people frustrated with always working on the same kind of task or technology? Is there a lack of knowledge sharing between team members?

If any of these sound familiar, then you will benefit from getting the right people doing the right things.

Of course, this is not just an ambition in the software world. All leaders have this goal, whether they are politicians, movie directors or…development team managers!

Intuitively it makes sense, but practically it is not always so easy to achieve. What gives one task a higher priority than another one? Is it the task that has been waiting the longest for attention? Or is it the task which someone is shouting the loudest for? And who is the right person to work on a given task? Is it the person who can complete it fastest? Or the person who needs to learn about that part of the system? Or the person who hasn't got anything else to do at the moment? These are the riddles all teams have to solve. And, as agile promotes the idea of delivering many smaller software changes more frequently (i.e. reducing batch sizes), it is a riddle that can become an acute daily challenge for teams that want to increase their agility.

In this chapter, I will explain:

- The three steps all teams need to take to prioritise work effectively
- How to do "just enough" prioritisation of work and why this is easier than many people think
- How to use *guided self-selection* so that people can choose tasks to work on that suit their interests and skills
- Why and how you can avoid key-person dependencies

PRIORITISATION

As I explained in the last chapter, one way of optimising for flow is to limit WIP (Work In Progress). One additional benefit of limiting WIP, is that it forces work to be prioritised. Once you agree that a team will work on no more than ten changes at any one time, then you are also accepting that sufficient prioritisation will need to take place in order to decide which ones those ten changes should be.

To ensure that effective prioritisation takes place, you need to take three steps:

1. Ensure that all requests for work are captured in one place. For software development teams this is often called the *backlog*.
2. Ensure that a mechanism is in place to prioritise this backlog before work is started on any of the items it contains[1].
3. Ensure that the team (and people on the team) are only asked to work on items in the backlog that have the highest priority.

The biggest challenge I consistently see teams facing relates to the last point. So often I hear stories of people dropping what they are working on if a senior manager comes to their desk with a request, a customer phones up with an issue, someone they know well presents them with an interesting requirement, or a host of other variations on these themes. This willingness to switch task is almost always born out of a desire to be helpful, or because the new task is perceived as being more important. But, in practical terms, it is impossible to ensure that a team is working on the right things, if work is directed to team members in an entirely ad-hoc way.

Understanding why team members are being approached directly is important. Often it is done out of frustration, feeling that if the "official" process is followed, the request will either never be completed or it will be unfairly "deprioritised" and take a very long time to get done. This is why the second point above is absolutely critical: having in place a fair, transparent, accessible and fast mechanism for requests to be added to the backlog and then prioritised against other requests.

I have seen that many teams struggle with prioritisation by trying to be too formulaic about it (for example, a priority 1 change must always take preference over a priority 2 change). In addition, many teams seek to prioritise requests "behind closed doors". This lack of transparency means that it is not possible for anyone outside of the team to understand how the prioritisation has been done.

One approach that I have found very effective is to gather the main "work giving" stakeholders together and have them agree the highest priority items for the team. Almost always, people engaged in such a discussion behave reasonably. For example, a project manager will understand that a major bug should be given priority over a feature they do not need delivered for several weeks.

Another approach that can work well is to give each stakeholder a quota. For example, maybe the product manager can choose five items, the service manager can choose three, whilst two are chosen by the development team for refactoring to reduce technical debt.

Another goal that many teams unnecessarily strive for is to try and have an entire backlog (that is changing daily) completely prioritised at all times. This is almost impossible to achieve (and can waste a lot of energy and time). It is just as useful (and much easier) to only do the amount of prioritisation that is actually needed. If the team needs to know which ten tasks to work on next, then all you need to do is figure out which ten are the highest priority. Often, it is quite easy to identify which are likely to be in the top 20, then remove any that can't be started yet (because they are dependent on another change, or still need to be agreed with the client). The top eight will probably be obvious and the bottom few will probably be obvious too. Leaving only a few at the boundary (in positions 8-12) that actually need to be prioritised with greater analysis.

Backlog

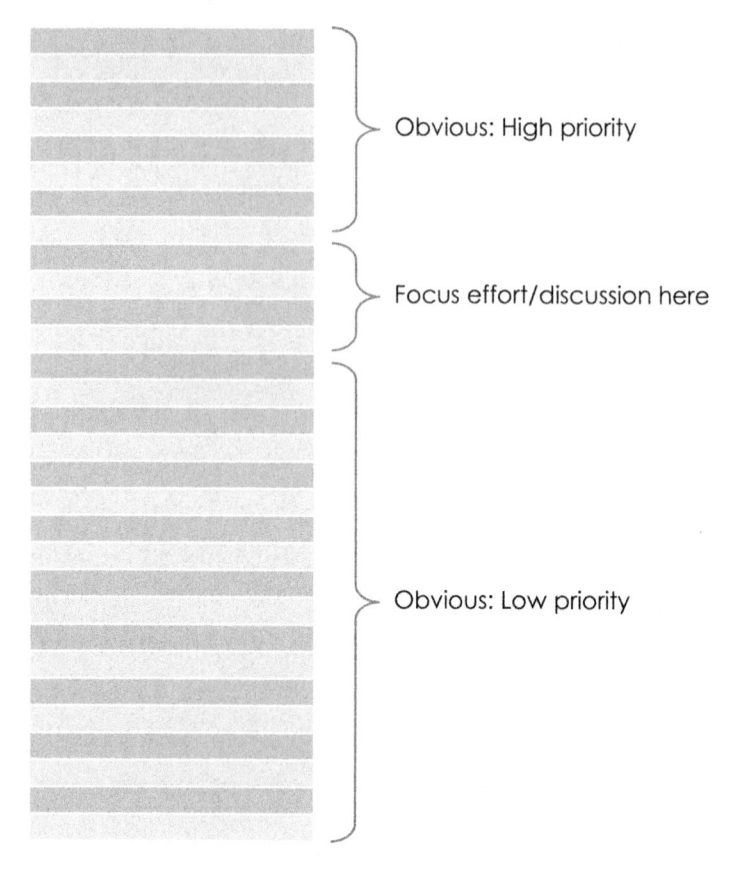

- Obvious: High priority
- Focus effort/discussion here
- Obvious: Low priority

A pragmatic approach to backlog prioritisation

Coaching Questions

- Do you have a single backlog maintained for the team?
- How are things added to the backlog?
- How is it prioritised?
- Do stakeholders outside the team understand how things are added to the backlog and do they perceive the prioritisation to be fair?
- Can the team add items to the backlog themselves (e.g. tasks to reduce technical debt)?
- Do stakeholders outside of the team try to give work directly to team members and, if so, why?

SELF-SELECTION

If your team successfully captures all requests for work in a single backlog, prioritises that backlog sufficiently, and ensures that attention is focussed on the highest priority items, you will already be outperforming most teams in terms of making sure that the right people are working on the right things. What's more, not only will they *actually* be working on the highest priority items, but they will also be *perceived* to be doing so by stakeholders outside of the team.

The final part of the puzzle is to get individual team members working on the activities that are best suited to them. What is best suited to any one member of the team is a complex question. It will depend multiple factors, including:

- **Their interests:** Do they have a passion for this feature? Are they keen to learn about this part of the system?
- **Their skills:** Do they know the needed programming languages? Do they know this part of the system well?
- **What other work needs to be done:** If everyone else needs to work on other features, maybe they need to pick this item up by default?

It might surprise you, but my experience is that enabling team members to use a structured approach to self-select what they will work on (something I call *guided self*-selection) is the most effective way of ensuring that this multitude of factors are properly considered and balanced.

A useful model that enables teams decide how to allocate work is described by Olac Maassen, Chris Matts and Chris Geary in their book Commitment (Maassen et al., 2016). They say that teams should aim to:

- Have no key-person dependencies
- Allocate team members with the fewest options first and those with the most options last

- Enable team members with the most options to coach and help those with the least options

Let's look at the issue of key-person dependencies first. I think everyone has at some point worked on a team that depends heavily on one or two experienced members of staff. They usually have a combination of strong knowledge about the software's functionality, as well as the technical skills needed to work on almost any part of it. They can complete work faster than others on the team, whilst simultaneously maintaining high levels of quality. This is good and it is valuable to the team (and the organisation), but it can create an unintended vicious cycle: more and more (especially complex) work ends up being allocated to them (because they will complete it faster and better than anyone else) which leads to their skills developing even more, whilst also denying other members of the team the opportunity to expand their skills and knowledge. Very quickly you end up with a key-person dependency: if they are not available for any reason, the team's capability to deliver work is disproportionately impacted. This can be a significant risk. The conclusion: sometimes it makes sense for people to take on tasks that will expand their knowledge and skills (even at the expense of speed or efficiency) in order to reduce key-person dependencies.

One way to do this, is to allocate the least experienced member of the team first. There will be fewer options for what work they can undertake (which is constrained by their skillset). Then you look at what work is left, and you allocate that to the more experienced team members (who will be able to tackle a wider variety of tasks). Try to get people working on tasks that will enable them to develop and broaden their skillset, not always the tasks most suited to their particular strengths.

The most experienced people on the team should not be allocated to specific tasks at all. Rather, they can help other members of the team by providing coaching, training, or supporting them in other ways.

At this point I would like to briefly touch on *cross-functional teams*. A cross-functional team is one that has all the skills needed to deliver and operate the product it is developing. However, there are also benefits in developing people to be more cross-functional themselves. Put simply, if everyone on the team can perform analysis, design, code, test or release tasks, then the team as a whole has a lot more flexibility to respond to peaks or troughs in demand in each of these areas.

Coaching Questions

- How is work currently allocated to people inside your team?
- Do you sometimes allocate work to people who are not the "most qualified" in order to increase knowledge sharing?
- Do you keep options open by allocating more experienced people last?
- Do the most experienced members of the team spend time training and coaching others?
- How cross-functional are the members of your team?

KEY TAKEAWAYS

- Capture all requests for work in a single backlog
- Do just enough prioritisation of your backlog so the team knows what is most important to work on next
- Make sure that how work is added to the backlog and how it is prioritised is transparent and visible to all stakeholders
- Use guided self-selection to allocate work
- Allocate work to avoid key-person dependencies: the most experienced people on the team should spend much of their time coaching and supporting others

FURTHER READING

***Commitment: Novel about Managing Project Risk* by Olav Maassen, Chris Matts and Chris Geary**

I've already mentioned this book. It is a quick and fun read (and it is the only agile book I know of that is presented as a graphic novel!). It is based around the concept of *Real Options* and the principles that:

- Options have value
- Options expire
- Never commit early unless you know why

These principles can be applied not only to the allocation of work on a team, but also to any situation where decisions need to be taken in fast-changing environments.

***How to Lead in Product Management: Practices to Align Stakeholders, Guide Development Teams, and Create Value Together* by Roman Pichler**

As I mentioned earlier, a full explanation of how to build and prioritise a backlog is beyond what I can cover in this book. I found that this book provides a good, modern treatment of the subject, which doesn't focus only on a mathematical ranking system, but rather on the interpersonal skills needed to successfully balance the needs of multiple stakeholders in an organisation.

REFERENCES

Maassen, O., Matts, C. & Geary, C. (2016). Commitment: Novel about Managing Project Risk. Hathaway te Brake Publications.

CHAPTER 3
AGILE SECRET #3: SHORTEN FEEDBACK LOOPS

WHY SHORTEN FEEDBACK LOOPS?

Does it ever feel like the same mistakes are made more than once? Do software changes not always deliver the intended benefits? Does it take a long time to diagnose and fix problems?

If any of these sound familiar, then you will benefit from shortening feedback loops.

In this chapter, I will explain:

- The four sources of regular feedback that every team needs about their product
- The difference between a customer and an end-user (and why getting feedback from both is important)
- How and why teams need a regular opportunity to

discuss and agree how they will improve the way they work
- Four tips for how to make sure that improvement suggestions actually get implemented
- The four metrics that every software team should measure

Broadly, there are two categories of feedback that I am going to cover in this chapter:

1. Feedback about the product itself, from software builds, testing, the customer, and end-users.
2. Feedback about how effectively the team is working, based on the team's own observations and on the metrics that they collect.

Frequently obtaining and making use of both categories of feedback is more valuable than doing so infrequently: shorter feedback cycles give you more opportunities to course-correct and usually reduce the amount and cost of any rework that may be required. One great way of achieving this is through the use of *information radiators*, which I'll also cover later. But first, let's look at the types of feedback that teams can get about their product and how they can make use of it more frequently.

FEEDBACK FROM BUILDS

As far back as 1996, the idea of a "Daily Build and Smoke Test" was being identified as a best practice [in Steve

McConnell's seminal work "Rapid Development: Taming Wild Software Schedules" (McConnell, 1996)]. Continuous Integration takes this a step further and ensures that every time a developer checks in some code, a full build of the software is performed together with some level of automated testing and, usually, some static analysis of the source code (to check for internal quality). The results of these builds must be quickly fed back to the team. Doing so enables many defects to be detected and fixed within minutes of them being introduced. It enables the team to determine if the internal quality of their codebase is remaining high. And it gives them confidence that they are never far away from having a potentially shippable product.

Coaching Questions

- How frequently do you build your software?
- How does the team receive feedback about these builds?

FEEDBACK FROM TESTING

I find it useful to think of testing as checking that the software works "as designed". In other words, does a feature work in accordance with what the development team envisaged when they started working on it. Simply put: is it bug free?

Traditional approaches to software development tended to conduct most of this software testing in one or more large batches towards the end of the development life-cycle. There were two reasons for this:

1. Software had to pass all tests before it could be released into production; after any changes (including to fix any bugs found in testing), all tests would need to be run again
2. Running the tests (mostly manually) required a large amount of time, effort and cost, so it made sense to run the tests as infrequently as possible

However, this approach also has two major downsides:

Firstly, it means that you have limited knowledge about how much progress you have made. You might believe that you are halfway through the coding (because all developers report that they are 50% complete, or because half of the features have been built) but, until testing has been performed to verify the quality of the work done so far, you cannot say with any certainty how much work is really left to do.

Secondly, with this approach, the time between a developer introducing a bug into the codebase and it being detected can be quite long (usually months). This makes finding and correcting the mistake much more difficult. By batching together multiple changes for testing, it is hard to know which one (and which developer) introduced the problem. Developers will have to cast their minds back several weeks or months to when they were working on the defective code, re-learning it sufficiently to be able to diagnose and fix the problem without introducing new issues[1].

Avoiding these downsides requires that tests are run much more frequently, ideally after every change a developer makes. For this to be feasible, the cost and time needed to run tests must be drastically reduced – this is where some level of test automation is critical. What is important to realise, is that the purpose of this test automation is not to replicate the traditional approach (running tests only a few times on a large batch of changes). Rather, test automation enables more frequent releases of reliable software and also provides rapid feedback about defects to developers. This rapid feedback gives you greater confidence in the progress you are making with developing the software and also reduces the time and effort needed to diagnose and fix issues as they are discovered.

Coaching Questions

- How frequently are software tests run and how soon do developers get feedback from them?
- If you do not run tests frequently, what are some of the reasons for this?

FEEDBACK FROM CUSTOMERS

With the testing I have just described, you will find out whether software performs as intended by the development team. However, what it doesn't tell you is that it works in the way that the customer was expecting.

Let me take a moment to be clear what I mean by a "customer". They are the person (or people or organisation) who have commissioned the development of some software (whether an entirely new product or some enhancements to an existing one). They could be internal or external to your company. They might be a product manager. Or they may be someone in the business who has identified a need that they believe can be met by developing some software. Sometimes customers are also the end-users of the software (for example, if a team of accountants commission new features for a financial reporting application that they use), but usually this is not the case (for example, the users of amazon.com do not request or pay for features to be developed on the website, even though they are the end-users of it).

Checking that software behaves in the way that the customer expected means giving them some way of testing it for themselves. In traditional approaches to development, this has often been called User Acceptance Testing (even though the people testing and accepting the software were rarely actually end-users) which was executed on a large batch of changes towards the end of the software development life-cycle.

As you start to release smaller increments of software more frequently, customer testing can occur more frequently as well. However, it is important to remember that the goal is to get feedback as soon as possible. With this in mind, a developer demonstrating a partially developed feature as they are coding it, is far better than waiting for feedback via some other mechanism in two or three weeks' time. Hand-drawing some wireframes of the user-interface in collaboration with the customer, or mocking up some screens before coding starts is an even better way to get feedback early. One team that I led, adopted the habit of developers picking up the phone to call the customer and talk through the requirement with them, before starting work on a change. This simple technique made it much more likely that features matched the customer's expectations first time.

At this point it's also worth briefly mentioning Behaviour Driven Development (BDD). In simple terms, BDD is about writing requirements that are human readable but that can also be compiled into automated tests. The idea is that the requirements that document the expected system behaviour (as expressed by the customer) are also used to verify the system behaviour. It is an important technique as it does, to some extent, enable the customer testing to be automated. However, in my experience, the single best way for customers to understand if software meets their expectations is for them to use it. BDD is a great complement to this (which has the added benefit of providing a structured approach to elaborating requirements and a way of automating their verification), but it is not a substitute for hands-on testing.

Coaching Questions

- Who are your customers?
- How does your team get feedback from them?
- Are you getting feedback from customers throughout the development life-cycle (including during design) or only after software is released?

Sometimes a customer checking that the software behaves as expected also equates to verifying that it delivers the desired benefits. For example, if the benefit that a customer is expecting from a change to a video editing package is support for 4k video, it is reasonably easy for them to validate that this benefit has been provided. Sometimes, however, the implementation of a feature does not automatically equate to the intended benefit being delivered. The customer may be expecting increased sign-up rates from a home page, or faster average call processing times in a call-centre. In these cases, testing that the benefit has been delivered will usually require that the software is put live in production and that some monitoring/logging is implemented which enables the benefit to be checked.

Sometimes A/B testing is used, where different end-users are exposed to different versions of the software (sometimes many different versions) to measure which one delivers the greatest value. An extension of this is Experiment Driven Development, where every feature is implemented as an experiment with clearly defined measurements that will determine if the feature is successful (and will be retained) or unsuccessful (and will be dropped).

Coaching Questions

- How do you evaluate that your software delivers the intended benefits?
- Are mechanisms built into your software to enable benefits to be tested and measured?

FEEDBACK FROM END-USERS

In many cases, crucial to anticipating whether or not the desired benefits will be achieved, is end-user testing. This can be performed (on a limited scale) before releasing software into production. It is also possible to release new features into production but to make them visible only to a small subset of users (for beta testing). Facebook makes new features available first only to internal employees before progressively rolling out to its full user base (Feitelson, Frachtenberg & Beck, 2013). An example I have seen in financial services is for new back-office processing systems to be enabled initially only for "friends and family" of employees. Both these approaches provide a relatively safe way to test the changes live in production by ensuring that the vast majority of users will not experience any negative impact if problems arise.

With these approaches, it is crucial that automated monitoring detects any anomalies/software crashes without users having to manually report them so that issues can be detected quickly and either rolled-back or fixed. It is also becoming increasingly commonplace to embed inside an application a way for a user to directly rate their experience and/or report any issues they are experiencing.

In addition to feedback about specific features or releases, it is incredibly valuable for the team to have empathy with the end-users of the software they are building. You can achieve this by ensuring that every single member of the team has direct and regular contact with actual end-users. Steve McConnell described the practice as a "near silver bullet", going on to say:

> "Putting developers in direct contact with users is an incredibly simple idea that is practiced far too seldom, yet it yields significant results whenever it is done." (McConnell, 2019)

Coaching Questions

- How does your team get feedback from end-users?
- Will your application monitoring automatically detect issues experienced by users?
- Do end-users have an easy and fast method for providing feedback?
- Does everyone on the team interact directly with end-users?

FEEDBACK ABOUT TEAM EFFECTIVENESS

The feedback I have covered so far has been feedback about the product itself. Does it work as designed? Does it behave as envisaged by customers? Does it deliver the intended benefits? And is the user experience positive?

However, another type of feedback is equally important: feedback about how the team itself is performing.

With this aim in mind, it is useful for teams to meet regularly with the explicit aim of understanding their own performance and seeking ways to improve it. A format for this type of meeting that has become common is to focus on three topics: what has gone well, what hasn't gone well, and what could be improved. These meetings are often referred to as *retrospectives*.

Coaching Questions

- Does your team have a regular opportunity to meet, review their performance, and think about ways to improve?

One approach, that worked really well for me with a team I managed, was to ask team members to write down on post-it notes their ideas for what had gone well, what hadn't gone well, and what could be improved. Then I would ask them to stick their ideas up on the wall. We clustered together similar thoughts and ideas and each one was explained by the person who wrote it, while others could ask questions. This made sure that everyone had a chance to air their views and opinions and that the discussion did not become overly dominated by one or two people.

This technique can be immensely beneficial for building team maturity. Enabling team members to identify what has been positive is a great way of ensuring that successes (however big or small) are recognised on a continual basis. I also found that, as we became accustomed to it, the idea that what hasn't gone well can be shared openly created a greater sense of trust, transparency and inclusivity within the team.

This may be surprising, but often, simply identifying issues led to improvements (without any specific discussion or action). When problems are shared, there certainly should be no fixed expectation that any further analysis must be performed in all cases or that a solution will always be found. As teams mature, identifying issues that have occurred becomes a low-cost, low-drama activity that is almost always beneficial in some way.

Once the team had written up their suggestions for improvement and stuck them on the wall, I would then use a technique known as *dot voting*[2] to select one improvement to be implemented before the next retrospective. We would often find that some suggestions were so straightforward or obvious that we could agree to go ahead with them in addition to the winner, usually with a quick "eye check" of the whole team.

Here are four additional tips to help you and your team select improvement suggestions and to make sure they get implemented:

1. **Treat improvement ideas as experiments.** Take an approach of "let's try this and, if it doesn't help, revert back or try something else", rather than treating the decision as binding on the team for eternity. This usually address most objections.
2. **Choose a manageable task.** With experience, teams will learn to propose feasible improvements. Rather than "re-architect the entire application"

people will suggest "re-factor that nightmare code module".

3. **Don't think of "no" as being forever.** Just like treating ideas that you do take forwards as experiments, ideas that are rejected today should not be banished forever. If they are still relevant at the next retrospective they can be proposed again and will be chosen if no other more useful ideas are forthcoming.

4. **Prioritise ideas that people are actually willing to implement.** Over time, team members will become used to proposing ideas that they will personally take ownership of. Rather than proposing that "someone" should refactor that awful code module, team members learn to propose that they will do it themselves (with support from the team as needed). Ideas that someone is willing to action immediately should always trump those for whom no owner is forthcoming. No matter what anyone says, no idea can be that important if no one is willing to invest their time in implementing it!

Although retrospectives are the main foundation of feedback on how agile teams are working, don't forget the value of having other feedback loops as well. Some of these should occur over shorter timespans, to uncover and unblock issues as soon as they arise. Others may add value if they take place over a longer time horizon, to allow for deeper reflection and a more strategic review of how the team is operating.

Coaching Questions

- In your retrospectives, is everyone's voice listened to?
- How do you decide which improvement suggestions to implement?
- Do improvements actually get implemented?

INFORMATION RADIATORS

The term "information radiator" is a general description of any method/tool for providing signals to the team about how they are doing. It might consist of a flat-screen showing the status of and statistics from the latest build. It might be a whiteboard showing the current status of changes being worked on. Or you can be more imaginative, such as a bell that sounds each time a successful build is completed. It is best to also provide other ways of notifying team members of important information in addition to having the information radiator (e.g. electronic notifications by email or in a chat channel). The reason that information radiators provide additional benefit beyond those other mechanisms is that they are constantly visible to the team and to passers-by. Even though the information can be accessed elsewhere, the psychological impact of displaying key data can be quite a significant motivator for the team. In this respect, information radiators provide transparency, encourage collaboration, and inspire teams to evaluate and improve their ways of working.

Coaching Questions

- What information radiators does you team currently have in place?
- What else could the team visualise and radiate?

METRICS

No discussion of feedback would be complete without a brief mention of metrics. There are four key metrics that almost all teams should collect and use to evaluate their performance and improvements. These are:

- Elapsed lead time to deliver valuable changes (from initial request to production)
- Frequency of deployments into production
- Change failure rate
- Time to restore service after a failure

These were explained by Nicole Forsgren, Jez Humble and Gene Kim in their excellent book "Accelerate" as the four metrics most highly correlated with improved business performance (Forsgren, Humble & Kim, 2018).

KEY TAKEAWAYS

- There are two types of feedback that are important: feedback about the product that is being built, and feedback about how effectively the team is working
- Short feedback cycles are better than longer feedback cycles
- Feedback about the product can come from a number of sources: software builds, software testing, customers, and end-users
- Feedback about how effectively the team is working should include an analysis of key metrics and regular opportunities for the team to reflect on their performance and propose improvements
- Information radiators are an excellent way to give regular and immediate feedback to the team

FURTHER READING

Continuous Delivery: Reliable Software Releases through Build, Test, and Deployment Automation by Jez Humble and David Farley

I still think this book contains probably the best explanation of Continuous Integration, with the bonus that it also shows you how to take this one step further and create a Continuous Delivery pipeline, where each build is automatically delivered into a production-like environment.

Accelerate: The Science of Lean Software and DevOps: Building and Scaling High Performing Technology Organisations by Gene Kim, Jez Humble and Nicole Forsgren

This is a modern classic and the de-facto standard for explaining which software development metrics correlate with better business outcomes. Not only will it help you decide what you should be measuring, but it also contains many other useful conclusions based on four years of extensive research.

REFERENCES

Baynham-Hughes, C. (2017). DevOps: Don't create the haystack. Retrieved from https://www.linkedin.com/pulse/devops-dont-create-haystack-chris-baynham-hughes/

Feitelson, D., Frachtenberg, E., & Beck, K. (2013). Development and Deployment at Facebook. Retrieved from https://research.facebook.com/publications/development-and-deployment-at-facebook/

Forsgren, N., Humble, J., & Kim, G. (2018). Accelerate: The Science of Lean Software and DevOps: Building and Scaling High Performing Technology Organizations. Trade Secret.

McConnell, S. (1996). Rapid Development: Taming Wild Software Schedules. Microsoft Press.

McConnell, S. (2019). More Effective Agile: A Roadmap for Software Leaders. Construx Press.

CHAPTER 4
10-MINUTE SCRUM OVERVIEW

OVERVIEW OF SCRUM

Scrum takes a time-boxed approach to software development. Each time-box is referred to as a *Sprint*. Each Sprint lasts the same amount of time and most teams choose a Sprint length of between two and four weeks.

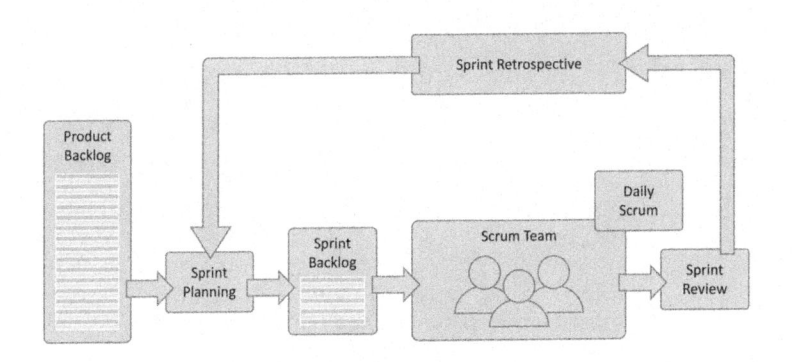

Overview of Scrum

Scrum defines a number of roles. A *Product Owner* is responsible for maintaining and prioritising a *product backlog*. At the start of each Sprint there is *sprint planning* session where the team agree with the Product Owner which changes will be delivered during the current Sprint (referred to as the *Sprint backlog*). Note that it is very typical for teams to describe the items in their backlog as *stories*. A *Scrum Master* is responsible for the day-to-day management of the team, with a focus on unblocking issues, rather than traditional task management. The *Scrum Team* will have all the skills (architecture, database, design, coding, testing) needed to complete the changes and deliver a potentially shippable product at the end of each Sprint. Typically, a stand-up meeting (called a *Daily Scrum*) takes place every day. At these meetings, team members report what they did yesterday, what they plan to do today, and any blocking issues they are experiencing or can anticipate.

As the Sprint progresses, the Product Owner remains available to the Scrum Team to quickly clarify any requirements. The Sprint ends with a *Sprint review* which consists of a demonstration to the Product Owner of the new features developed during the Sprint. This demo often includes other stakeholders such as customers and end-users.

During Sprint planning, the team estimates the size of each change that they accept into the Sprint (usually in *story points*). At the end of a Sprint they check which changes were completed in full and add together the total story points for those changes (only counting fully completed ones). This tells the team their *Sprint velocity* for the Sprint that has just been completed. Measuring their Sprint velocity enables the team to decide how many story points it will be realistic to deliver in future Sprints.

Before starting the next Sprint, the team will hold a *Sprint retrospective* meeting where they analyse what went well, what didn't go well, and what they could do to improve their ways of working in the future.

WHY SCRUM WORKS

Scum optimises for flow because:

- The whole team focuses on delivering the changes committed to for the current Sprint which maximises touch time.
- Batch sizes are limited to what can be delivered inside one Sprint.
- The team re-organises itself around the work to alleviate bottlenecks.
- Blockers are detected quickly via daily scrums and the Scrum Master has a responsibility for facilitating their resolution.
- Teams make use of automated testing[1] to deliver a potentially shippable product in every Sprint. This, together with the close contact with the Product Owner and regular demos (Sprint reviews), reduces the amount of rework that is needed.

Scrum ensures that the right people work on the right things because:

- The Product Owner has responsibility for ensuring that the highest priority items are chosen for the next Sprint.
- Team members self-organise around the work (facilitated by the Scrum Master and the Daily Scrums).

Scrum shortens feedback loops because:

- Automated software builds and testing give developers regular feedback that they are close to a potentially shippable product and that they have not broken any features developed in previous Sprints.
- Regular interactions with the Product Owner and demos (especially when they include customers and end-users) give the team feedback about whether their changes are meeting the intended needs.
- Retrospectives provide a structured and regular method for the team to evaluate and improve its ways of working.
- Many Scrum teams have a physical board or screen as an information radiator showing the status of tasks being worked on in the current Sprint.
- As a minimum, Scrum teams measure their Sprint velocity (how many story points they deliver in a

Sprint) and they also know how frequently they will have a potentially shippable product available (i.e. the length of their Sprints).

As you can see, Scrum is a fantastic out-of-the box solution. Now you understand not just how to implement Scrum, but also how its different components work together to achieve the principles of agility explained in the previous chapters. When all the components are not in place, there are some common problems that can occur. In the next chapter I cover the top five mistakes I have seen people make with Scrum, so that you can avoid them.

FURTHER READING

The Scrum Guide: The Definitive Guide to Scrum by Ken Schwaber and Jeff Sutherland

Written by the creators of Scrum, this book has been made available for free and can be downloaded from scrumguides.org. It is short, accessible and accurate. It is an excellent place to start with finding out more about the Scrum method.

Succeeding with Agile: Software Development Using Scrum by Mike Cohn

Considered by many to be the definitive textbook on implementing Scrum, this comprehensive guide covers Scrum in depth and provides highly practical advice for implementing it within an organisation (with some advice for scaling).

CHAPTER 5
5 SCRUM MISTAKES TO AVOID

MISTAKE #1: WATER-SCRUM-FALL

Forrester coined the term Water-Scrum-Fall to describe cases where companies implement Scrum for the coding activities (and usually detailed design and unit testing as well) but they do the pre-coding activities (such as requirements analysis and architecture) and the post-coding activities (system testing and release) in large batches before and after the Scrum process. There can be many reasons why this occurs. Sometimes it relates to the organisation structure: testers may all belong to a central team meaning that system testing cannot be managed inside a Sprint. Sometimes it is because there is a commercial need to define all the requirements up-front. Or sometimes there are other constraints, such as system testing being an expensive manual process and hence there being a desire to minimise the number of times it is performed (and certainly not do it every Sprint).

Unfortunately, this type of Scrum implementation significantly reduces the level of agility that is achieved. Although batch sizes for part of the process remain small, the end-to-end process still operates in large batches. The Scrum team can't reorganise to alleviate bottlenecks that exist outside of the team, and it can often be hard to unblock any issues that are not within their direct scope of control. The Product Owner cannot re-prioritise work easily or address new customer requirements, as much of the work is performed up-front. The lack of system testing and/or acceptance testing during every Sprint means that the developers receive feedback far less frequently (and means that what they build during each Sprint may not truly be potentially shippable). And the ability for the team to improve via regular retrospectives is limited to the small part of the end-to-end process that they have control over.

MISTAKE 2: MULTI-SPRINT STORIES

One challenge often faced when implementing Scrum, is how to break-down software development tasks so that they are sufficiently small to be completed inside a single Sprint. Effective Scrum relies on having:

- Short Sprints (usually 1-4 weeks). Longer Sprint lengths increase the batch size and reduce the opportunities for feedback.

- Stories that can be demonstrated (and potentially released) at the end of each Sprint. Usually this means avoiding stories that do not have a visible outcome. Individual tasks (such as writing a database abstraction layer) may be necessary in order to deliver a story, but they cannot be stories by themselves; if they are not demonstrable, then they inhibit the team's ability to get feedback.

Given these constraints, it can be hard to define stories that are both small enough to be completed inside a (relatively short) Sprint, but also big enough to be demonstrated.

Faced with this challenge, sometimes teams choose to split stories across Sprints. For example, they might do the story's design in one Sprint, the coding in the next Sprint and the testing in a third Sprint. Unfortunately, this approach brings with it the same problems as long Sprints or non-demonstrable stories: batch sizes are increased and feedback cycles become longer as effectively neither are constrained by the Sprint length.

In summary: the concept of delivering a fixed set of demonstrable and potentially shippable software development entirely within one Sprint is fundamental to how Scrum makes a team agile.

MISTAKE 3: INEFFECTIVE PRODUCT OWNER

Scrum neatly solves the challenge of correctly prioritising work by placing responsibility for this with the role of the

Product Owner. In addition, the Product Owner is responsible for providing quick feedback to the development team about any questions arising about how features should be implemented.

In practice, finding someone who has the time, skills and authority to do this role effectively can be challenging. Very often I have seen that:

- **Product Owners can struggle to prioritise the backlog.** It is not unusual to find Product Owners who are acting as a proxy for multiple stakeholders and, therefore, correct prioritisation can require a great deal of consultation and diplomacy. Sometimes the Product Owner does not have sufficient authority to make priority calls and stick to them. I have even seen cases where others in the organisation will seek to circumnavigate the Product Owner by giving tasks directly to members of the Scrum Team.
- **Product Owners may find it difficult to provide feedback to development teams.** They may simply not have sufficient bandwidth to respond to queries fast enough. But also, just like for prioritisation, they may not be sufficiently empowered. If, when a developer raises a query, the Product Owner must seek feedback from multiple stakeholders before responding, then the developer will not get a reply fast enough and tasks will tend to get blocked "waiting for

feedback" which reduces touch-time and makes the team's velocity slower and less consistent.

MISTAKE 4: NOT REACHING A POTENTIALLY SHIPPABLE STATE IN EVERY SPRINT

Although the exact definition of "potentially shippable" in Scrum varies somewhat, most would agree that it implies some level of quality assurance has been completed. Usually at least some level of unit, integration and system testing, as well as some feedback from the Product Owner about what has been built. And although most would say it is acceptable if some further steps are still required before the software can go-live (for example, certification for compliance purposes), the principle is that, at the end of a Sprint, you are confident that no significant rework or additional effort will be required before it can go into production. Doing this means that you are never more than a few weeks away from being able to release what you have developed so far. If development has progressed more slowly than anticipated, it provides you the option to release (the most important features) on time, or to release the scope you had originally planned but slip the release date.

The most common cause I have seen for not reaching a potentially shippable state in every Sprint is an over-emphasis on *coding* activities and an insufficient emphasis on *quality control* and *validation* activities.

MISTAKE #5: IGNORING REQUIRED TECHNICAL PRACTICES

Martin Fowler coined the term FlacidScrum to describe a Scrum implementation where insufficient attention has been given to the technical practices that are needed to make Scrum successful (Fowler, 2009). Many people consider Scrum to be purely a software *management* method: it defines key roles and a process for how work is done. However, my experience matches Martin Fowler's observation: it is practically impossible to implement what Scrum mandates without certain technical practices in place. In particular, many of the problems I have already described will occur if there is insufficient automation of software builds and testing.

REFERENCES

Fowler, M. (2009). FlacidScrum. Retrieved from https://martinfowler.com/bliki/FlaccidScrum.html

CHAPTER 6
10-MINUTE KANBAN OVERVIEW

OVERVIEW OF KANBAN

Kanban, as a method for improving the agility of software development, was first described in 2010 by David J. Anderson in his book "Kanban: Successful Evolutionary Change for Your Technology Business" (Anderson, 2010).

The starting point for implementing a Kanban system is always your existing way of working. Implementing Kanban uses a process known as STATIK (Systems Thinking Approach to Implementing Kanban). In summary, the steps of this process are as follows:

- **Understand sources of dissatisfaction.** Who is unhappy about how things are done currently? What are they unhappy about?

- **Analyse demand and capability**. What types of work do the team have to deliver? Is the demand constant or does it have peaks and troughs? Is the team managing to meet the current (and anticipated) levels of demand?
- **Model the work-flow**. What are the value-adding steps that each work-item has to go through? For many software teams these may be similar to the software development life-cycle steps I described in Chapter 1. But many software development teams also have other types of work to do, such as preparing estimates or diagnosing production issues.
- **Discover classes of service**. For almost every team, there will be a need to provide a different level of responsiveness for some work-items compared to others. For example, usually a major production fault must be worked on with higher priority than a new feature for which the deadline is still several weeks away. Kanban refers to these differing needs as different *classes of service*.
- **Design the Kanban system and visualise**. The work of the team is visualised (usually via a physical or virtual *Kanban board*) which shows the current status of all work that the team has in-progress. Work In Progress (WIP) limits are agreed to explicitly constrain the amount of work that the team will take on at any one time. Policies are also agreed and documented for how work enters the

system and how it moves from one step to the next.

This may all seem quite abstract, so let's consider an example Kanban board. In this example, the team works on changes after a functional and technical design has already been prepared, and they take the changes from that stage all the way through to their release into production.

Backlog	Selected 4	Code 6	Review 6	Release Build 12	Regression Test 12	Release 12	User Acceptance 12	Done

Example Kanban board

As you can see, the Kanban Board has a column for each step in the process. For every work-item that the team is working on, a post-it note with the name of that work-item is placed in the column that describes its current status. As work is completed, post-it notes on the board move from left to right.

Most of the column headings have a number underneath them. This is the agreed WIP limit for that step in the process. It means that everyone has agreed, for example, that there will never be more than six changes being coded at the same time, or there will never be more than twelve in one release. You will see that the first and last columns do not have a WIP limit: any number of changes can be in the backlog or be accepted by users as complete.

All the columns that do have WIP limits represent the part of the process for which overall WIP is being constrained. It is for this part of the process that the team will also capture key metrics (for example, lead time and change throughput). Note that the metrics are meaningful precisely because the WIP is limited. Think of it like this: the average lead time to complete a task for someone working on twenty tasks in parallel will be longer than for someone focussed on only one task. By setting the WIP for the team, the metrics for lead time and throughput will tend to stabilise.

Whenever I have seen a system like this implemented, it always leads to immediate improvements. The introduction and visualisation of WIP limits stimulates teams to identify and resolve blocked work-items (rather than simply starting on new ones). The WIP limits also encourage team members to help out with any tasks where there is a bottleneck: if someone can't start a new change because twelve other changes have not been regression tested yet, then they will be minded to help complete the regression testing. A popular phrase used by Kanban practitioners is "Stop starting, and start finishing!"

Part of setting up a Kanban system is defining the policies for how work items move from one column to the next. Often, these policies are called *Definitions of Done* (or *Definitions of Ready* when they describe pre-requisites needed before the team will start work on an item) and are a way of building quality into the process to reduce rework. A policy of particular importance is the one that governs how work items are added into the system (in this case, how do they move from the "Backlog" column into the "Selected" column). A common approach is for there to be a *queue replenishment meeting* where stakeholders agree which items from the backlog will be the priority to work on next. Note that the WIP limit of four for the "Selected" column does not mean that four items will be selected at each replenishment meeting. If there are still two items in the "Ready" column from last time, then only two new ones can be selected and added.

The combination of limiting WIP and controlling how work is allocated to the team, often enables team members to focus much better on one task at a time. Every time someone must switch from one task to another, overheads are introduced: saving the work for the current task, opening the work for the new task, and then re-familiarising yourself with where you got to with it last time. Not only do these overheads take time (and therefore reduce efficiency), but they also make it more likely that mistakes will be made. I know that I am much more prone to making errors if I am having to switch frequently between different activities! This is why, when the introduction of a Kanban system lowers WIP and reduces interruptions, productivity and quality improve.

Kanban also recommends a number of other regular meetings. In particular, there is usually a daily stand-up meeting around the Kanban board. At these stand-up meetings, someone on the team will take the lead and *walk the board* from right to left, with a focus on work items that are closest to being completed and on detecting any blockers. Kanban also suggests one or more meetings where the operation of the system is discussed, and improvement ideas are considered for implementation.

What you may have already realised, is that Kanban can be applied to Scrum. If the team is currently practicing Scrum, then Kanban can be implemented (just as it would be for any other current way of working). In this case, the Sprint planning meetings would be the queue replenishment meetings, WIP would be set by the Sprint velocity, and daily scrums and Sprint retrospectives would map onto the Kanban review meetings. In fact, many organisations who start with Scrum, later choose to overlay Kanban onto it as a way of driving further improvements. This is an approach known as Scrumban (which can be a confusing term, as it is not a mixture of the two methods as the name might suggest, but rather it describes the specific case where Kanban is implemented when Scrum is the existing way of working).

WHY KANBAN WORKS

Kanban optimises for flow by reducing WIP which leads to:

- Smaller batch sizes
- A higher proportion of touch time to wait time
- The identification and alleviation of bottlenecks and blockers

In addition, the creation and evolution of explicit Definitions of Done help to reduce rework.

Kanban ensures that the right people work on the right things because:

- There is an agreed mechanism in place to determine what the team should work on next
- Team members self-organise around the work, often reaching the stage of being able to select work items themselves based on agreed policies (i.e. that a high priority change should be chosen in preference to a low priority change)

Kanban maximises feedback in an indirect but very powerful way. In general (although some Kanban experts disagree about this point), work items only move from left to right. This raises the question of what happens when a change enters user acceptance and a bug is identified? Surely then the change has to move back to the "Code" column? Most Kanban practitioners agree that the change should stay in the "User Acceptance" column (as user acceptance is the *dominant knowledge discovery activity* that is being performed). It also drives an important behaviour for the team: new changes can't be started until previously worked on changes have been completed. And, in this case, completed means released into production and accepted by the customer.

By contrast, I once encountered a team who were incentivised by the number of changes they completed (as well as how fast they completed them). However, any fixes to bugs found (even those discovered in system testing) had to be raised as new changes. This meant that the team were recognised as performing well, regardless of how many bugs were found in system testing, acceptance testing, or even in production. In fact, their measured performance (in terms of lead time and throughput) would actually be boosted by delivering buggy software quickly. Well designed Kanban systems incentivise teams based on the end-to-end operation of the software delivery lifecycle, not just their part of it.

The Kanban board should be located in a place that is visible to the whole team (and to passers-by), even if a virtual board is being used. The Kanban board acts as an important information radiator which visibly indicates to people inside and outside the team what is being worked on, which members of the team are working on what, and which work items are blocked.

A core part of Kanban is measuring the performance of the system and then trying to find ways, as a team, to improve this performance by adapting how you work. In particular, teams look for ways to reduce the lead time and increase throughput.

Just as with Scrum, Kanban has to be implemented quite carefully to achieve the expected benefits. In the next chapter I cover the top 5 mistakes I have seen people make with Kanban, so that you can avoid them.

FURTHER READING

Essential Kanban Condensed by David J. Anderson and Andy Carmichael

David J. Anderson first developed the Kanban method for managing software development and Andy Carmichael has also been at the forefront of its evolution. This book gives an up-to-date description of the state-of-the-art of Kanban which is concise and clearly written.

Kanban from the Inside by Mike Burrows

This is now the de-facto textbook for Kanban which explains the method through its values, foundational principles, and core practices. It also explains other important models that are required for successful Kanban implementations (such as Systems Thinking, Theory of Constraints, and Lean Startup). It ends with detailed advice for how to successfully implement Kanban for a team.

REFERENCES

Anderson, D. J. (2010). Kanban: Successful Evolutionary Change for Your Technology Business. Blue Hole Press.

CHAPTER 7
5 KANBAN MISTAKES TO AVOID

MISTAKE #1: TASK-BOARD ONLY

One of the most noticeable parts of many Kanban implementations is the Kanban board itself. It often represents the only physical change in the working environment, and it is the place where daily stand-ups occur. It is also the natural place for other discussions about progress to take place. What's more, for many teams, the shared view of what the team is working on at any one time brings significant benefits.

However, implementing Kanban properly requires more than only visualising the workflow on a physical board. If WIP is not limited, then batch sizes can continue to be large, blocked work-items can remain blocked, bottlenecks can be hard to identify, the proportion of touch time will not improve, and any metrics collected will be somewhat meaningless (and certainly highly variable). If a clear mechanism for how work is added to the system from the backlog is not agreed, then the team may not work on the right things. And if Definitions of Done are not documented and refined for each step, then high levels of rework may continue to be required.

MISTAKE #2: NOT LIMITING WIP

There can be some resistance to limiting WIP when first introducing a Kanban system. Although Kanban is a "start with what you do now" approach, one of the few changes it does require is the establishment of WIP limits. Managers often worry that implementing them may reduce staff utilisation (even though, as I explained in Chapter 1, for most teams the benefits in term of productivity will far outweigh any small reduction in utilisation). Stakeholders who allocate work to the team may fear any mechanism that limits their right to pile work onto the team, and they will need to be reassured that it is far better for the team to complete the tasks allocated rather than simply accepting any work (even if it ends up being completed very slowly, badly, or even abandoned).

What has also surprised me, is that sometimes members of the team find the idea of WIP limits uncomfortable. Some people attach a certain status to their long "to do list", seemingly feeling that it demonstrates how busy they are and, therefore, how important their knowledge and skills must be to the organisation. Some will not like the idea that they may have to shift their focus towards unblocking problematic work items rather than simply switching to work on fun new ones. And others may simply be concerned that if WIP is limited, they might not have enough to do (a scenario that I have never once seen materialise in practice). Limiting WIP also makes it much easier to see exactly what everyone is working on and some may find this clarity uncomfortable.

All these reactions are reasonable and understandable. However, my experience (and that of many other Kanban practitioners) is that agreeing to limit WIP at the outset is an important factor for the success of a Kanban implementation. It can be hard to set the correct WIP limit at the beginning, but remember it can always be adjusted. A good rule-of-thumb that is often acceptable to most stakeholders as a starting point is two work-items per person plus a few more. Don't worry if it feels like you are setting the WIP limit so high that it won't have an impact. It is far better to start with a WIP limit (even a high one) than to not agree a WIP limit at all. It can always be adjusted in the future.

MISTAKE #3: NOT STARTING WITH WHAT YOU DO NOW

When you start by identifying sources of dissatisfaction, and later you model the workflow, it is incredibly tempting to try and design a better process than what you actually do today. Resist this urge!

Part of the power of Kanban is that it minimises resistance to its implementation because it starts with what you are doing already. Most people can agree that better visibility of the process and clearly documented policies are a good thing. And most can be persuaded of the value of limiting WIP.

If you start to optimise the process before you implement Kanban, then there is a high likelihood that resistance to the change will increase (because you will be trying to change people's ways of working). What's more, as you may not have any baseline metrics for how you operate today, no one (including you) will know whether your "improvements" were beneficial or not.

A core principle of Kanban is that improvements are identified and implemented iteratively and collaboratively by the team. To do this, the Kanban system first must be setup based on the current ways of working and some baseline metrics collected. Then the team can try improvements. If they bring benefits then the team keeps them. If they don't bring benefits, the team can roll them back and try something else. Understand this and you will understand why David J. Anderson sub-titled his book "successful *evolutionary* change for your technology business" (Anderson, 2010).

MISTAKE #4: NO FEEDBACK LOOPS

Fundamental to Kanban is the idea that you visualise what you do currently, measure the performance of the system, and then seek to optimise that performance (taking an experimental and evolutionary approach). If the Kanban board is not clearly visible to the team, or if metrics are not being collected and shared, then there is unlikely to be much effective feedback or improvement going on.

Without this ongoing feedback and improvement, Kanban reduces down to doing exactly what you do currently, and it is unlikely that you will see much increase in agility[1].

MISTAKE #5: MAPPING WHO DOES THE WORK RATHER THAN THE VALUE-ADDING STEPS

A common misunderstanding when setting up a Kanban system is to think that the columns on the Kanban board represent the person (or team) doing the work, rather than the value-adding activity that is being performed. Of course, for many teams, the way they currently operate may mean that the columns do map on to specific roles. In our example, perhaps regression testing is always performed by a separate test team, or release activities are always performed by an operations team.

Thinking carefully about the value-adding steps that a work item goes through rather than which person, role or team performs the activity is an important part of understanding the different types of work teams are performing, how end-to-end value is being created, and what classes of service are required.

The psychology of focussing on the workflow rather than who performs it is important. Over time, I have often seen teams reorganise the way they work spontaneously. I have seen cases where developers will help out with release activities, or project managers will help with testing, because they can see from the Kanban board that spending their time on those tasks (rather than remaining narrowly focussed on their own role) will improve overall team performance. If people perceive that the columns on the Kanban board represent roles, then they may be inclined to let the people with that "role" sort out a blocker or bottleneck, rather than offering to do something about it themselves.

CHAPTER 8
HOW TO CHOOSE BETWEEN SCRUM AND KANBAN

I have a confession to make: you're going to find this chapter very short and rather obvious! That's because you now know the three agile secrets from Chapters 1-3. You also know the basics of Scrum and Kanban and the mistakes to avoid (covered in Chapters 4-7). Armed with this knowledge, choosing between Scrum and Kanban is straightforward.

In fact, you now have the skills to make an informed choice about any method, including frameworks for scaling agile (such as SAFe and LeSS).

No method is superior to others in all cases. It is always context dependent (including the skills and enthusiasm of the people who will be making the change). It is also true that any method implemented well will beat any other method implemented badly.

Now, you can figure out which methods will work best for you by weighing up how they will help you optimise for flow, get the right people doing the right things, and shorten feedback loops.

Having said that, here is my best advice for the main reasons to adopt either Scrum or Kanban.

WHY CHOOSE SCRUM?

Scrum is a good candidate when some or all of the following are true:

- There is no existing way of working (e.g. you are bringing together a new team)
- You already have (or can find) someone to be the Product Owner who will be capable and empowered to do the role effectively
- It will be feasible to complete changes entirely within one Sprint (with Sprints being no longer than 1 month)
- It will be extremely rare that the content of a Sprint will have to be changed mid-way through (for example to fix urgent bugs in production)
- It will be possible to have sufficient technical practices in place from the outset. As a minimum, you will need to have substantial automated test coverage and Continuous Integration
- The required team size is not too large (usually fewer than ten people)

- It will be feasible to have a truly cross functional Scrum team (that won't be reliant on testers, analysts, architects, etc. from outside of the team).

WHY CHOOSE KANBAN?

Kanban is a good candidate when some of all of the following are true:

- There is already an existing way of working in place (which is, at least to some extent, formalised)
- The team serves multiple stakeholders (e.g. there are multiple "work givers")
- There is sometimes a requirement to handle emergency requests (that wouldn't be able to wait for the next Sprint of a Scrum team)
- Work-items usually require people from more than one team to work on them before they are complete

SCRUMBAN – THE BEST OF BOTH WORLDS?

As I covered in Chapter 6, Kanban can be applied to Scrum. Doing this is known as *Scrumban*. With it, you first implement Scrum, and then you use this as the starting point for further evolutionary improvement using Kanban. The name Scrumban is a bit confusing, as it implies that it somehow merges the two methods together. This is not the case: you start with Scrum, then you implement Kanban over it to drive further improvements.

My advice is, if it makes sense for you to adopt Scrum, start there. Once you have done that, I see no reason why any team wouldn't benefit from then adopting Kanban on top of this.

On the other hand, if it will be hard to adopt Scrum (e.g. there is already a deeply embedded existing way of working, changes can't be completed within a Sprint, you can't put the required technical practices in place from the outset, etc.), then I would ignore Scrumban and go straight to Kanban instead.

CHAPTER 9
5-MINUTE AGILITY SELF-ASSESSMENT

HOW TO ASSESS YOUR TEAM'S AGILITY IN 5 MINUTES

In 2019, together with Chris Baynham-Hughes, John Chatterton, Panagiotis Tamtamis and Dan Usher, I created an open-source online DevOps Maturity Assessment tool (which has since been forked on GitHub over 60 times). I have used that as the basis for the self-assessment questions in this chapter.

To use this self-assessment:

- Answer yes or no to each question
- For any question where you answer "no", think about how your team could improve

For each question, I also give you a suggestion for what might be a "quick win" and, in most cases, what might be a longer-term change worth considering.

But remember: I can't tell you (and neither can anyone else) what will give the biggest benefits in your particular situation. Having read this book, you are the person who is best qualified to understand what needs to change and to decide what actions to take next.

SELF-ASSESSMENT QUESTIONS

Q1: Does your team have a new, potentially shippable, version of the product available every 1-2 weeks?

- **Quick win:** Reduce the batch sizes for post-coding steps in your development process (such as system test and release).
- **Longer term:** Implement Continuous Integration (including some level of automated regression testing).

Q2: Does your team track the following metrics: elapsed lead time to deliver valuable changes (from initial request to production), frequency of deployments into production, change failure rate, and time to restore service after a failure?

- **Quick win:** Capture and share any of these metrics that are easy to collect, even if you can only do it monthly (rather than in real time) and even if they will be indicative rather than fully accurate. Anything is better than nothing!
- **Longer term:** Implement tooling to automatically capture and radiate these metrics in real time.

Q3: Does your team regularly meet to discuss what is working well, what isn't working well and what they can improve, and are the top improvement items implemented?

- **Quick win:** Have a 1-hour retrospective with your team at least every month. Use my tips for running retrospectives in Chapter 3 to make sure that you always commit to implementing one improvement.

Q4: Does your team take actions to ensure that they do not create or experience bottlenecks with/for other teams?

- **Quick win:** Make any blocked items visible to the whole team.
- **Longer term:** Collect data about blockers to identify common problems/patterns. Feed this into your retrospectives to uncover ways to reduce their occurrence and/or negative impact.

Q5: Are any work items that are blocked swiftly identified and then people collaborate to rectify the situation?

- **Quick win:** Check for blocked items during short, daily team meetings and agree who will take action to unblock them.
- **Longer term:** Limit Work In Progress (WIP) to encourage the team to resolve blockers in preference to taking on new tasks.

Q6: Is there a clearly defined mechanism for prioritising the backlog?

- **Quick win:** Create a backlog (if you don't already have one) and setup a regular meeting with stakeholders who provide work to the team to do the minimum necessary prioritisation.
- **Longer term:** Talk to work-giving stakeholders outside of the team to uncover how work should be prioritised and what classes of service are required.

Q7: Does the team work on the highest priority items in the backlog?

- **Quick win:** Make it visible to the team which are the most important items in the backlog that should be worked on next.
- **Longer term:** Discuss and agree with your team how they can self-select work.

Q8: Are the most experienced team members allocated to tasks last so they can be free to focus on the most business critical or complex problems and help others develop cross functional skills?

- **Quick win:** Allocate less work to experienced team members (e.g. 50% of their current work load).

Q9: Does the team have fast feedback loops in place from testers (at least every day), the Product Owner (at least every 3 days), customer (at least every 2 weeks) and end-users (at least every 2-weeks)?

- **Quick win:** Introduce the practice of everyone on the team spending time interacting with end-users.
- **Longer term:** Introduce Continuous Integration with automated testing after every build (with results notified to the whole team). Introduce regular demonstrations of new features to the product owner, customer, and end-users.

Q10: Are there proactive steps taken to ensure there is no major dependency on "superheroes"?

- **Quick win:** Allocate work using the approach described in Chapter 2 to reduce key-person dependencies.
- **Longer term:** Implement code review and pair programming practices (if you don't do these already). Even if not used for all development work, they can significantly improve knowledge sharing amongst the team.

CHAPTER 10
RECAP OF COACHING QUESTIONS

Just to be absolutely clear: there is nothing new here! This chapter simply brings together in one place the 55 coaching questions covered in Chapters 1-3 to make it quick and easy for you to refer to them.

OPTIMISE FOR FLOW

Flow efficiency:

- If you don't already have it, can you make a list of the main steps that a software change goes through in your organisation to go from the initial idea right through to it being live in production?
- Can you find out or estimate your team's flow efficiency (ratio of touch time to lead time)?
- What are some of the main causes of wait time that you can identify?

- Are handovers between different teams exacerbating wait time?

Batch processes:

- Can you identify where the large batch transfers occur in your end-to-end software delivery process?
- Are they before small batch processes?
- Do they lead to queues?
- How could you reduce these batch sizes?

Work In Progress (WIP):

- Do you already track the WIP of your team?
- If not, can you measure or estimate your team's current WIP levels?
- Is it more than 2-3 changes per person?
- If so, what are the main causes for it being higher?
- Could you experiment with introducing WIP limits?

Bottlenecks:

- Do you have an idea of where the bottleneck in your software development life-cycle might be?
- How could you confirm or disprove this?
- Can you think of how your team might alleviate the bottleneck in your process?
- Can you think of one or more ideas in each

category of exploit, subordinate and elevate (from the Theory of Constraints)?

Blockers:

- How does your team currently manage blockers?
- Is this approach effective?
- Are blockers resolved swiftly enough?
- What frequently occurring source of blockers exists for your team?
- What could you change to reduce the delay caused by these sources of blockers in the future?

Rework:

- Can you estimate what percentage of time your team spends on rework?
- How could this rework be avoided?
- How could you shorten feedback cycles so that the cost of rework is lowered?

GET THE RIGHT PEOPLE DOING THE RIGHT THINGS

Backlog management:

- Do you have a single backlog maintained for the team?
- How are things added to the backlog?
- How is it prioritised?

- Do stakeholders outside the team understand how things are added to the backlog and do they perceive the prioritisation to be fair?
- Can the team add items to the backlog themselves (e.g. tasks to reduce technical debt)?

Allocating work:

- Do stakeholders outside of the team try to give work directly to team members and, if so, why?
- How is work currently allocated to people inside your team?
- Do you sometimes allocate work to people who are not the "most qualified" in order to increase knowledge sharing?

Key-person dependencies:

- Do you keep options open by allocating more experienced people last?
- Do the most experienced members of the team spend time training and coaching others?
- How cross-functional are the members of your team?

SHORTEN FEEDBACK LOOPS

From software builds:

- How frequently do you build your software?

- How does the team receive feedback about these builds?

From testing:

- How frequently are software tests run and how soon do developers get feedback from it?
- If you do not run tests frequently, what are some of the reasons for this?

From customers:

- Who are your customers?
- How does your team get feedback from them?
- Are you getting feedback from customers throughout the development life-cycle (including during design) or only after software is released?
- How do you evaluate that your software delivers the intended benefits?
- Are mechanisms built into your software to enable benefits to be tested and measured?

From end-users:

- How does your team get feedback from end-users?
- Will your application monitoring automatically detect issues experienced by users?
- Do end-users have an easy and fast method for providing feedback?

- Does everyone on the team interact directly with end-users?

About team effectiveness:

- Does your team have a regular opportunity to meet, review their performance, and think about ways to improve?
- In your retrospectives, is everyone's voice listened to?
- How do you decide which improvement suggestions to implement?
- Do improvements actually get implemented?
- What information radiators does you team currently have in place?
- What else could the team visualise and radiate?

NOTES

1. AGILE SECRET #1: OPTIMISE FOR FLOW

1. For the sake of simplicity, in this example I am assuming that one requirement equates to one feature which equates to one software change (in practice such a one-to-one mapping is rare).
2. "Touch time" is also commonly referred to as "process time" or "processing time"

2. AGILE SECRET #2: GET THE RIGHT PEOPLE DOING THE RIGHT THINGS

1. An in-depth discussion of the techniques for actually deciding the relative priority of items in the backlog is outside the scope of this book. However, good prioritisation is critical to achieving the desired outcomes from software development, and I would encourage you to learn more about the disciplines of Product Management and Portfolio Management.

3. AGILE SECRET #3: SHORTEN FEEDBACK LOOPS

1. See also Baynham-Hughes (2017)
2. For a brief explanation of dot-voting, see https://www.nngroup.com/articles/dot-voting/

4. 10-MINUTE SCRUM OVERVIEW

1. Some would argue that automated software builds and testing are not, strictly speaking, part of Scrum. However, I have found that, practically, it is very difficult to meet the requirement of Scrum to have a potentially shippable product at the end of every Sprint without these practices in place.

7. 5 KANBAN MISTAKES TO AVOID

1. Technically, implementing a Kanban system will, even without any visualisation or evolutionary change, impose some kind of WIP limits. Practically speaking, these WIP limits alone always yield some benefits.

ACKNOWLEDGMENTS

I would like to dearly thank Chris Baynham-Hughes and Catherine Lequibain for their invaluable review, feedback and discussion about early drafts of this book – the final result was immeasurably improved by your input!

I would also like to thank the numerous engineers, managers, agile coaches and executives who I have worked with over the years. Those experiences led to the insights that I have captured here.

I would also like to give special thanks to Johanna Rothman, who generously shared with me her advice for how to write and publish a book.

Finally, a warm thank you to Allan Kelly for telling me to "ship it" and reminding me that releasing a short book with actionable content is better than a long book that no one reads!

ABOUT THE AUTHOR

With over 20 years of experience in tech, David's passion is how innovative technology solutions can enable new experiences, business models and operational efficiencies.

He has implemented Agile/DevOps within traditional, fixed-price environments and coached other teams to do the same. He is a Fellow of the British Computer Society, a Chartered IT Professional and a regular public speaker who has a passion for showing how new approaches can produce better results.

He co-authored the book Deliberately Digital: Rewriting enterprise DNA for enduring success – a handbook for enterprise-wide digital transformation, and has also written numerous thought leadership papers and blog posts.

You can reach David on:

- Twitter: twitter.com/daviddalywl
- LinkedIn: linkedin.com/in/daviddaly-fbcs-citp

Or contact him by email on david@daly.uk

Printed in Great Britain
by Amazon